CLB 1363
Published in Great Britain 1985 by Crown Books.
Crown Books is a registered imprint of Colour Library Books Ltd.
© 1985 Illustrations and text: Colour Library Books Ltd.,
    Guildford, Surrey, England.
Filmsetting by Acesetters Ltd., Richmond, Surrey, England.
Produced by AGSA, in Barcelona, Spain.
Printed and bound in Barcelona, Spain by Rieusset and Eurobinder.
ISBN 0 86283 322 1

ENGLAND
FROM THE AIR

CROWN BOOKS

First port of call for today's visitor from Europe, Canterbury (previous pages) was journey's end for generations of pilgrims, and now marks the beginning or end of days-long hikes for downland walkers. The soaring spires of its impressive cathedral mark and distinguish the city to the traveller on the ground, and even from the air dominate the huddle of thousands of lesser buildings which appear to be kept at bay only by the definitive, encircling road system. Charles Dickens passed through on his way to Broadstairs (these pages) to take up residence in the castellated Victorian house on the cliff edge (top right). Here he wrote *David Copperfield*, while the building itself, despite its proximity to the bright, sandy sweep of the bay, inspired another novel, *Bleak House*.

From Kent, the route into London may take you over Tower Bridge (overleaf). Confident and ornate, it leads to the cradle of London's post-Conquest history – the Tower itself. Flanking this superb, beautifully preserved legacy of the past are reminders of the present: the edges of the bustling density of the City's commercial centre (left), and the beginnings of the residential sprawl of the East End's former docklands.

'Ships, towers, domes, theatres and temples...' Wordsworth would hardly recognise London today, save for the wide, serene passage of the Thames through its very heart (previous pages). Bridges are indispensable: Tower Bridge in the foreground, then London Bridge, Southwark Bridge (beyond the railway viaduct), Blackfriars and, distantly, Waterloo. In a confusion of landmarks, the cylindrical Telecom Tower stands out, but spotting St Paul's, or even the Tower of London, might defy a latter-day Wordsworth. From another angle, however, St Paul's retains its traditional scenic mastery (these pages); the buildings which surround it or provide its backdrop lack its stateliness, and it still commands the view from the river.

Further west up-river lies the Palace of Westminster, shown (overleaf) in the throes of a massive cleaning programme to rescue it from the grime of 140 years – still evident on the Victoria Tower (right) – and to restore its former buff-coloured clarity of line and detail. Westminster Hall, last rebuilt under Richard II, sits resolutely out of square to the rest of the complex, while across the road, supported by its decorative flying buttresses, stands Westminster Abbey, the setting for the coronations of most of England's monarchs for over nine hundred years.

Those elderly gentlemen in scarlet coats and black tricorn hats, pottering contentedly around London, reside in arguably the most famous 66 acres in London – Chelsea's Royal Hospital (previous pages). Brick-built to Sir Christopher Wren's design by 1692, its quiet grandeur is enlivened by stone window-dressings, cornerstones and portico. Along the site's north front runs the road that bears its name – Royal Hospital Road – and which separates it from the gardens and residential area of South Kensington (top left). Immediately west of the Hospital is the National Army Museum.

Hampton Court Palace (these pages) was enlarged in the late 17th century, and the mark of Wren is again immediately evident in the tall, square extension to the old Tudor structure. A rabbit-warren of a palace, the original bristles with brick chimneys, turrets and castellations – an apt memorial to the ostentatious Cardinal Wolsey who built it. Formal Restoration landscaping emphasises the dual personality of the Thames-side site. Landscaping of a different sort brings hundreds of thousands to London's Kew Gardens each year, where educational and recreational benefits abound. Dotted by their magnificent hothouses (overleaf), the three hundred acres provide a welcome breathing space amid the expanding London conurbation.

One of the most celebrated of many sporting sites on London's fringes, Wimbledon (previous pages) is the headquarters of the All England Lawn Tennis and Croquet Club. For two weeks each year, its two dozen grass and hard courts echo to the sound of ball upon racquet, the stentorian call of umpires, and the applause of thousands of devotees of world tennis. Centre Court, and Court No 1, each with comprehensive spectator facilities, dwarf the others, but the sunny luxuriance of green overall never fails to recall that inimitable fortnight of delights, from strawberries to silver trophies.

Twenty miles further south-west lies Guildford (these pages), with its steeply rising High Street virtually bisecting this photograph laterally. Among the most classic Georgian main streets in the south of England, its pride and joy is the huge clock suspended over it from the side of the 17th-century Town Hall. Of Guildford's more modern landmarks, the post-War cathedral sits grandly aloof on elevated ground to the west.

Meanwhile, Bodiam Castle (overleaf) stands proudly in is moat, almost anachronistic among the careful lines of the modern rural Sussex landscape. A tribute to the earliest attempts to combine residential comforts with military defence, it seems the perfect, most regularly proportioned of English medieval castles.

Some thirty miles to the north-west of London lies the quiet village-town of Marlow (previous pages). The epitome of fashionable Buckinghamshire, its spacious riverside gardens and leisurely through-traffic of Thames sailing-craft endow it with a placid, timeless and still very rural charm.

A further thirty miles north-west is England's educational capital – Oxford (these pages) – with its 'dreaming spires and pinnacles'. The bold, 14th-century spire of St Mary the Virgin (centre foreground) faces the squat Oriel College on the opposite side of the 'High', and vies with the burgeoning dome of the Radcliffe Camera (now a library). Between them rises All Souls College with its immaculately tended quadrangle. William of Wykeham's slightly larger New College – one of the first built in Oxford – lies by Hertford College, where students are enjoying the midday sun in the oak-dominated courtyard. Queen's College stands to the right of New.

One dreaming spire is enough for Salisbury (overleaf), in neighbouring Wiltshire: its cathedral boasts the tallest in England – at 404 feet – as well as the most complete, unadulterated medieval design. Its square, tree-lined close gives residents of the adjacent North and West Walks admirable vistas, and marks a break between the main city (right) and the suburbs of Harnham, along with the wide expanse of pasture where the Nadder (top left) joins the Avon.

A trio of seascapes in England's rich and varied south-west peninsula. A typical south Devon mixture of smooth, sandy bays and rocky outcrops meets the aerial eye at Bigbury-on-Sea (previous pages). The sandbar connecting the cliffed island with the mainland is covered during rough weather, while the meandering estuary offers shelter for small shipping. The South-West Coastal Path which has run westwards from Poole Harbour passes through to skirt the south-west tip of England and follow the north coast of Cornwall and Devon to Minehead.

St Ives Bay (these pages) rewards the hiker's pause, with obvious natural and recreational attractions that have made this north Cornish town a flourishing seaside resort for decades. Despite close-packed development, there is charm in the colourful juxtaposition of bleached yellow sands, aquamarine seas, a dark patchwork of fields and the characteristic slate-grey of the houses.

A more expansive effect awaits further up the coast near Newquay, where the vast, flat beach of Fistral Bay (overleaf) blends into the sloping rock leading to Towan Head. The headland's high rock-faces make it an explorer's delight; footpaths across it and round its very edges testify to the fascination of rugged cliffs and crashing waves below.

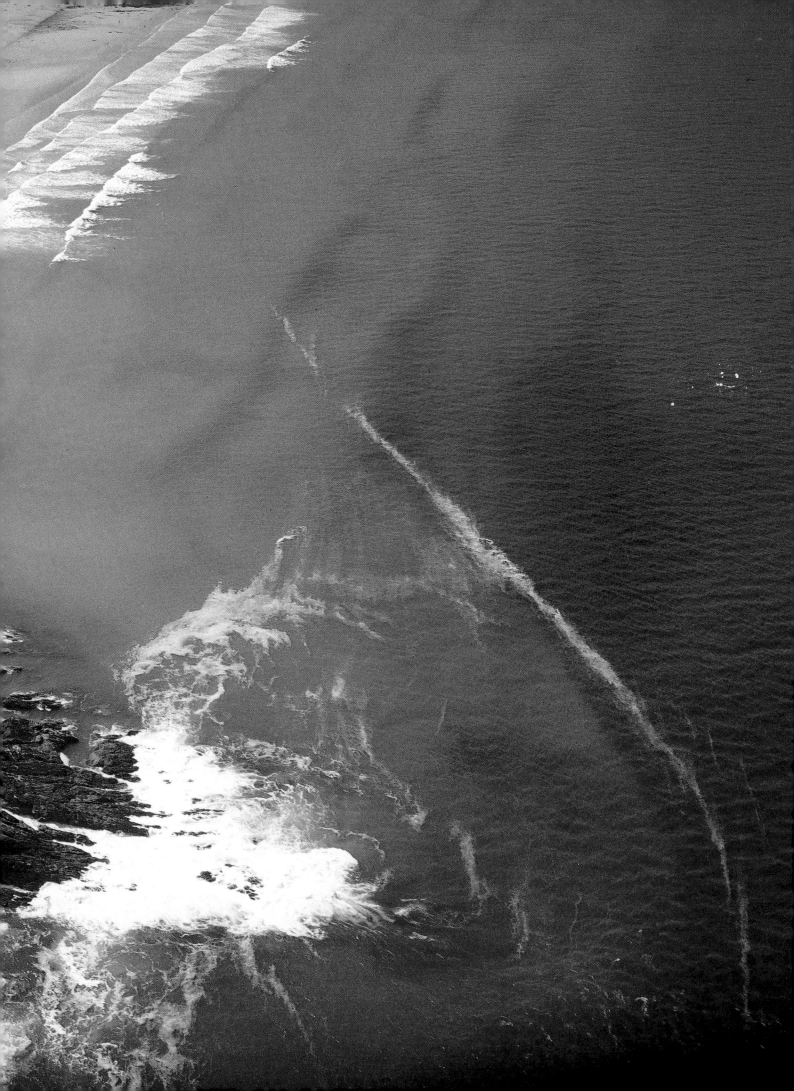

Think of natural springs, the Romans, and miles of Georgian residential architecture, and you think of Bath. Many of this rivetting city's 18th-century buildings appeared when the spas the Romans had put to such good use were revived to render Bath instantly fashionable as a place at which to take the waters. Its centre (previous pages) is a thrill. The Avon, sturdily banked, flows through under the fine, triple-arched Pulteney Bridge, to the right of which four elaborately-roofed pairs of terraces come together at Laura Place. With variety, from its perpendicular-style Abbey (left) to its 20th century county cricket ground (right, centre), Bath has something for everyone, and the space to enjoy it in.

As charming in its own way is the small Herefordshire town of Ross-on-Wye (these pages). In truth, it barely touches the river, and then only in the environs of its picturesque, 12th-century church, St Mary's, with its graceful, slender spire. Most of Ross dates from the 1600s, and was built around the splendid, arcaded Market Hall (right foreground) which is still its physical and spiritual heart.

Travel due east for Bourton-on-the-Water (overleaf), miraculously unspoiled by its enormous, decades-long popularity. Even on the greyest day, its warm, Cotswold stone dwellings defy the seasons.

The 12th-century town plan of the original Stratford-upon-Avon (previous pages) – three streets parallel with, and three at right-angles to, the river – remains unchanged despite successive rebuilding and continuing development. Meanwhile, the 18th-century spire of Holy Trinity, the riverside church where Shakespeare was baptised and is buried, proclaims the modern community's link with the bard. Further up-river stands the Royal Shakespeare Theatre – a solid, 1930s structure, complete with picture gallery and museum, which replaced a Victorian predecessor destroyed by fire.

Centrepieces in vastly-industrialised Coventry (these pages) are the old and new cathedrals: the flat-roofed building designed by Basil Spence and completed in 1962 (centre) has a clear-glass west screen affording worshippers sight of the bombed shell of the old, with only its Gothic spire and pentagonal sanctuary remaining.

Between Stratford and Coventry lies the fine old town of Warwick (overleaf), guarded on the Avon by its medieval castle in one of Capability Brown's sweeping landscaped settings. In the centre of the town the Norman church of St Mary, mostly rebuilt around 1700, sports a pseudo-Gothic tower – an attempt by its restorers to retain the medieval flavour of the original.

In the 1950s redevelopment of Birmingham's city centre began (previous pages) – a difficult undertaking if disruption of the lives of over a million people was to be avoided. Most of that work is now complete and, for all its inevitable density, the city offers an enviable combination of commercial and industrial opportunity. Access is a priority, with swingeing ring-road systems and two main stations – New Street (far left) and Moor Street (centre foreground) – in the heart of the scheme, close to the famous Bull Ring Centre (bottom left).

But to get away from it all you could do worse than travel north to Rydal Water (these pages) in the southern Lake District. A paradise for fell-walkers and short-distance ramblers alike, the area is alive with the sights, sounds and smells of nature virtually untouched by man. Elevated woodlands (right) support fir, oak, birch, beech and sycamore, and offer superb views of the lake with its main feature, Heron Island. Beyond lies its neighbouring lake, Grasmere, and the village of that name is just visible to the right. The wilder attractions of Helvellyn (overleaf) await the northbound traveller; its broad, masculine surface (left) is highlighted by fine winter snow, while the waters of Thirlmere reflect the raw climate of the heart of Lakeland.

The magnificent hilltop cathedral at Lincoln (previous pages) is visible for up to forty miles of the surrounding, flat, rich fenland. Its Norman origins match the Conqueror's castle beyond, while its ornate Gothic architecture is as impressive within as without. The Bishop's Palace, to its left, watches over the old Roman town, while the lower ground is dominated by Victorian development (left), and the uphill plateau by more modern building (right). Beyond lies the Carholme, where for years the Lincoln Handicap was run to begin the flat-racing season.

Well south of Lincoln, Oxford's rival university, Cambridge (these pages), is compact yet uncrowded. The River Cam winds between successive colleges – St John's (top left); then Trinity; King's, with its towering, pinnacled chapel (centre); and Queen's. With its liberal complement of churches, chapels, museums, fine terraces and busy, well-facilitated shopping centre, Cambridge possesses universal appeal.

Across to the east stands one of England's most exquisite stately homes – Holkham Hall (overleaf), owned by the Earls of Leicester for 250 years, and built to harmonise with the graceful, barely undulating Norfolk landscape. Reminiscent of some Italian palace, its Palladian design and formal gardens recall an age of luxury and elegance. Once again, the aerial view perfectly demonstrates the blend of the works of man and nature which gives England such enviable and satisfying landscapes.

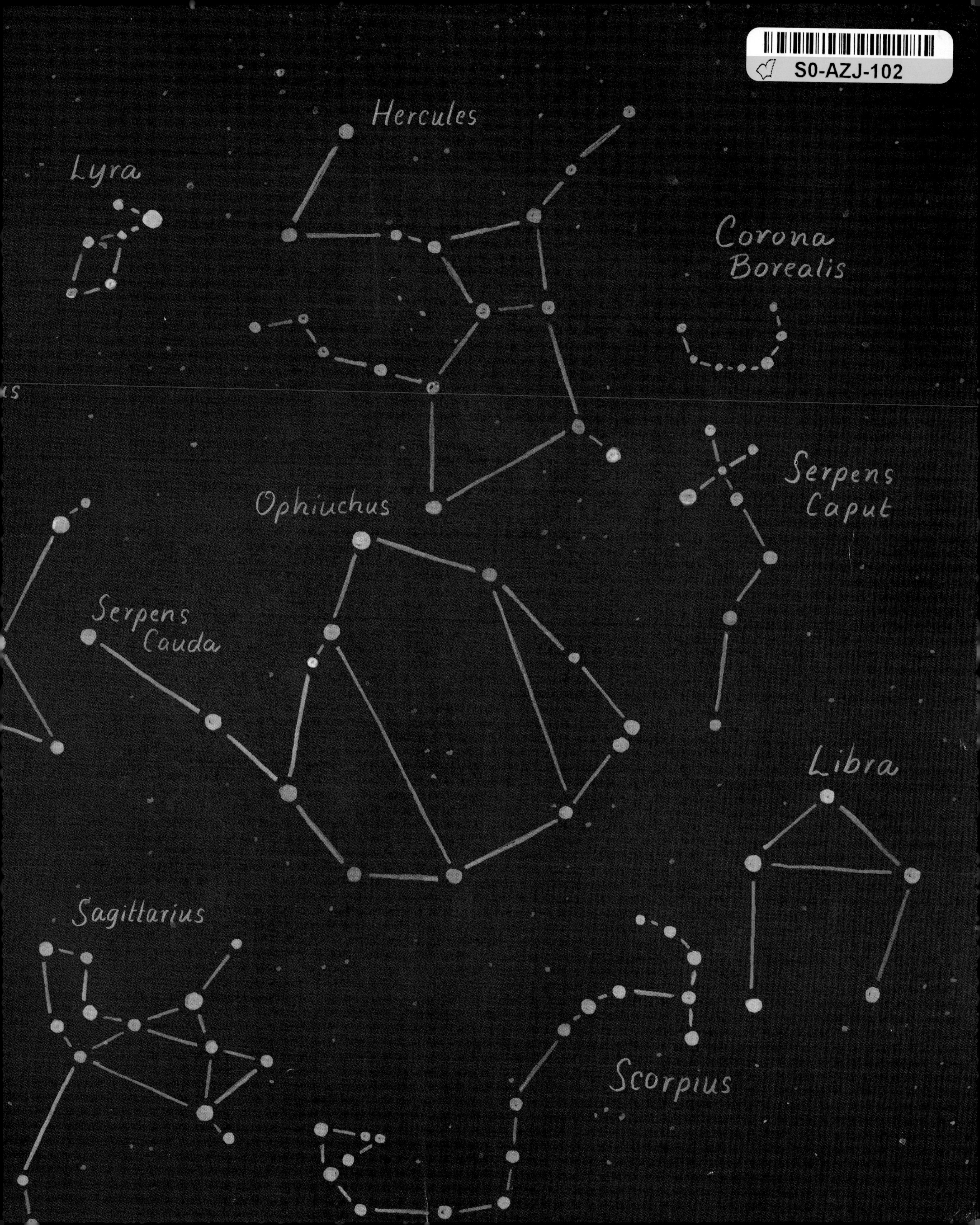

Lyra

Hercules

Corona
Borealis

Serpens
Caput

Ophiuchus

Serpens
Cauda

Libra

Sagittarius

Scorpius

In loving memory of my father, Saul Blumenthal,
who lived life afire with learning —A.B.M.

To Ava —E.H.

Text copyright © 2019 by Alice B. McGinty
Jacket art and interior illustrations copyright © 2019 by Elizabeth Haidle

Visit us on the Web! rhcbooks.com

Educators and librarians, for a variety of teaching tools, visit us at RHTeachersLibrarians.com

Library of Congress Cataloging-in-Publication Data is available upon request.
ISBN 978-1-5247-6831-7 (trade)
ISBN 978-1-5247-6832-4 (glb)
ISBN 978-1-5247-6833-1 (ebook)

The text of this book is set in Belen.
The illustrations were rendered in inks, in graphite powder, and digitally.

MANUFACTURED IN CHINA
2 4 6 8 10 9 7 5 3 1
First Edition

THE GIRL WHO NAMED
PLUTO

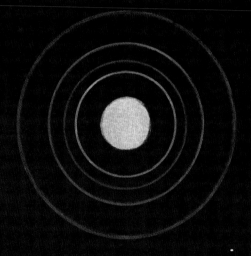

The Story of Venetia Burney

WRITTEN BY
Alice B. McGinty

ILLUSTRATED BY
Elizabeth Haidle

schwartz & wade books · new york

Out of the classroom, down the hallway, and out the door—Venetia Burney and her schoolmates follow their teacher, leaving their British schoolhouse behind. It is the year 1930, and they are counting their steps from the sun, a circle drawn on their classroom blackboard.

"Thirty-nine, forty, forty-one," Miss Claxton leads, her words as precise as her footsteps.

At exactly forty-one paces from the sun, they lay down a bird seed: Mercury.

At seventy-seven paces, they place a pea: Venus. Next, a larger pea: Earth.

After placing a bead for Mars and an orange for Jupiter, the largest planet, they stop at 1,019 paces, inside University Park. There, they lay down a golf ball: Saturn.

There are two more planets in the solar system, Uranus and Neptune, but Miss Claxton tells her students that they are too far away. She will let their imaginations finish the planet walk.

Saturn

Uranus

Neptune

1,019 paces from the sun

When Venetia and her friends return to the park
later with lumps of clay for the planets, they run,
counting paces to Mercury, Venus, Earth, Mars,
Jupiter, Saturn . . . all the way to Neptune.

MERCURY

VENUS

EARTH

MARS

Venetia's imagination whirls, trying to fathom the real distances. She has memorized each number. Stormy blue Neptune orbits 2.79 billion miles from the sun. And what lies beyond? How far does the solar system reach?

Venetia brings her questions to breakfast each morning, and Grandfather Madan answers as many as he can.

She and Mother have been living with Grandfather since Venetia's father died. Old and stately like the Oxford library where he was head librarian, Grandfather knows that questions lead to learning. And his family is afire with learning.

Along with the planets, Venetia is learning about Greek and Roman gods. When she reads about Mars, the Roman god of war, she is reminded of her great-uncle, Henry Madan, a science master who named the two moons orbiting that planet. He chose Phobos and Deimos, Mars's twin sons. Moons and planets named from legends—what a marvelous link between science and story!

At breakfast one Friday, as Grandfather sifts through the newspaper, he starts to read aloud:

"A NEW PLANET: DISCOVERY BY LOWELL OBSERVATORY
Professor Harlow Shapley announced today that the Lowell Observatory at Flagstaff, Arizona, had discovered a ninth major planet. The planet, which has not yet been named, is beyond Neptune."

A new planet! Venetia leans forward in her chair. Another lump of clay to add to their model!

"I wonder what it should be called," Grandfather says, his brow creased.

Venetia's imagination takes off, flying, leaping, connecting the dots from science to story. She knows that this planet, so far from the sun, must be frozen, dark, and lifeless. It would be like the underworld— the underworld ruled in Roman myths by Neptune's brother, Pluto.

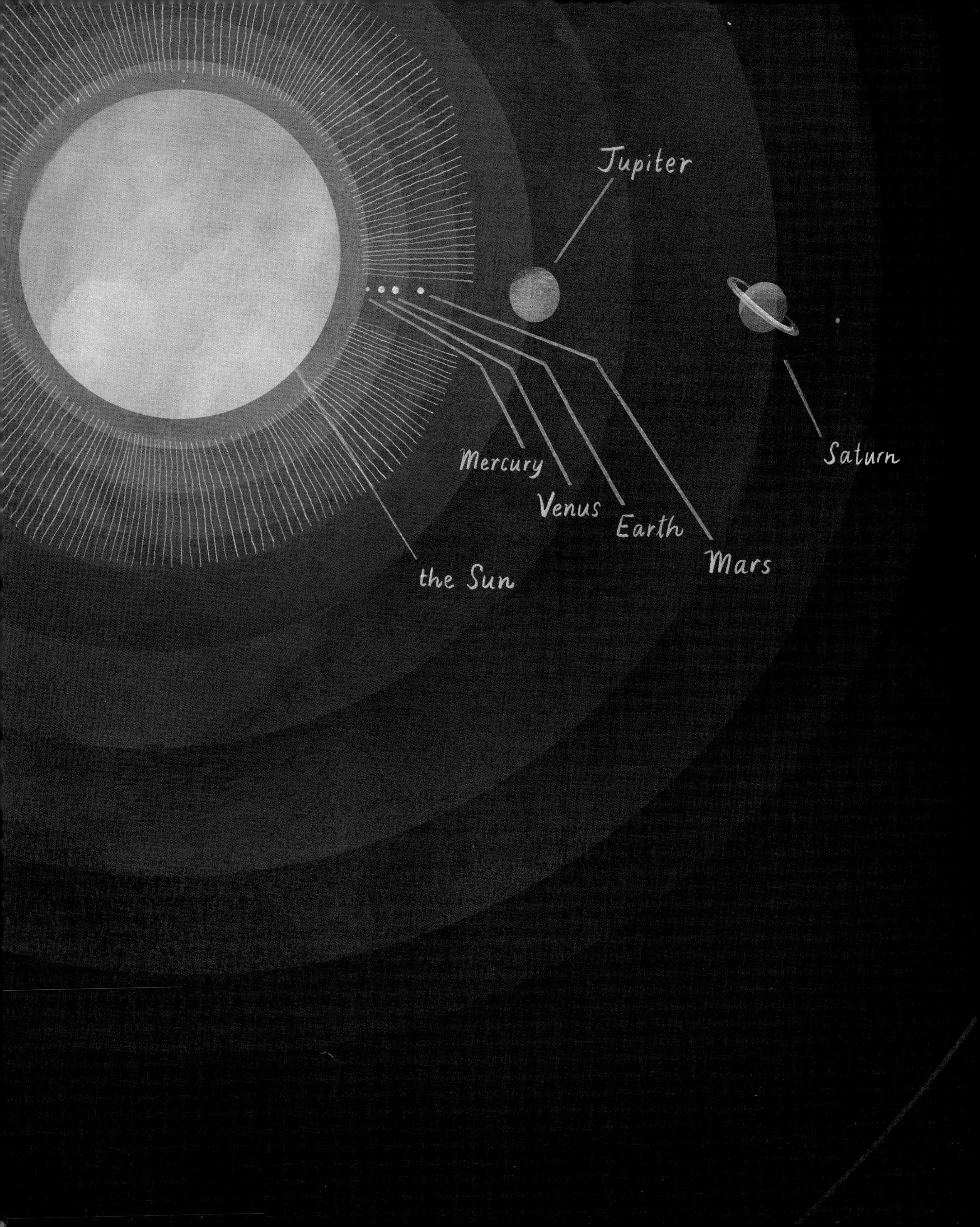

Jupiter

Saturn

Mercury

Venus

Earth

Mars

the Sun

Uranus

Neptune

"It might be called Pluto,"
Venetia says.

Grandfather's eyes widen. He loves the name!

He tells Venetia that he'll share her idea with his friend,
Professor Herbert Hall Turner of the Royal Astronomical Society.
Perhaps he has a say in the decision.

After Venetia leaves for school, Grandfather writes this note:

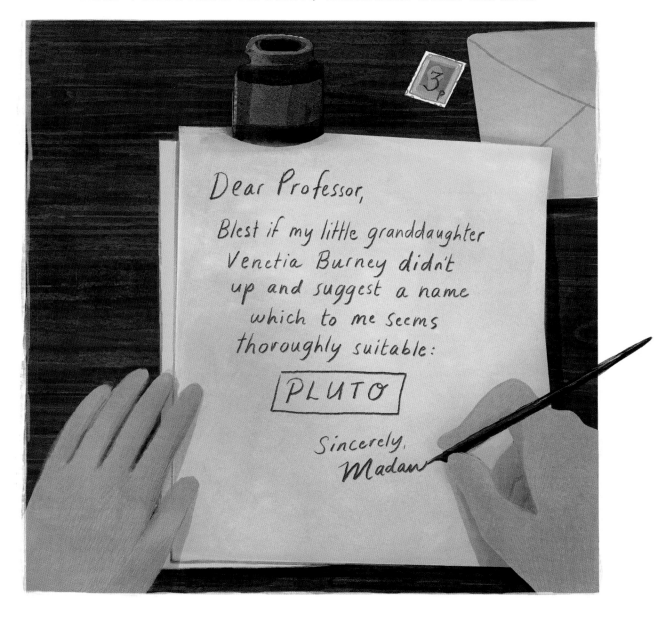

> Dear Professor,
>
> Blest if my little granddaughter Venetia Burney didn't up and suggest a name which to me seems thoroughly suitable:
>
> PLUTO
>
> Sincerely,
> Madan

On his way to the library, Grandfather drops off the note at the professor's home.

Meanwhile, not far away, Venetia and her schoolmates are buzzing with excitement about the new planet. They fire question after question at Miss Claxton.

Miss Claxton promises to find out.

That evening, Venetia lies in bed, her mind adrift with Planet X. In the flurry of her thoughts spins one name: Pluto. Could it be the name for the new planet? Were the astronomers deciding now?

Saturday morning dawns, and Venetia and Grandfather
search the papers for more information about Planet X.
Mostly, though, they wait to hear from the professor.

That afternoon, a response arrives.

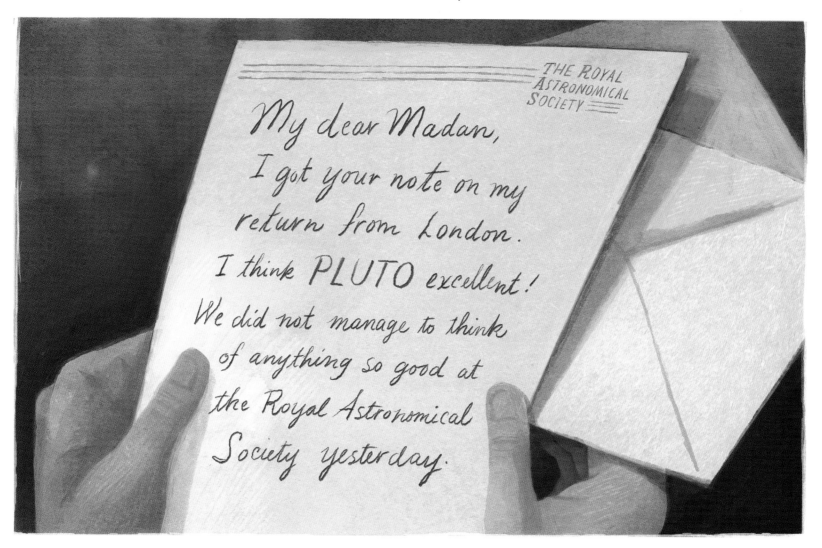

THE ROYAL
ASTRONOMICAL
SOCIETY

My dear Madan,
I got your note on my
return from London.
I think PLUTO excellent!
We did not manage to think
of anything so good at
the Royal Astronomical
Society yesterday.

The professor's note goes on to say that he has written to the astronomers at Lowell about Pluto. It will be up to them to decide.

A week goes by.

At school, Venetia works on lessons in math, science, and history.

At home, she and Grandfather keep busy—reading, playing,
and waiting. Will the astronomers like her idea?

March turns to April. And Venetia waits.

April drags on. Outside, the trees sprout leaves. And Venetia waits.

If Venetia could see what was happening across the ocean, she would find that PLUTO has made its way through the doors of the Lowell Observatory to Clyde Tombaugh, the shy assistant who discovered Planet X.

OXFORD,
ENGLAND

EUROPE

His first choice for a name? Pluto. Not only is it a perfect fit for
this dark, icy world, but the first two letters are *PL*, the initials of
astronomer Percival Lowell, who began the search for the planet.

Finally, at the end of the month, the astronomers vote. It's unanimous. The ninth planet will be named Pluto.

When Grandfather shares the news with
Venetia, she beams, her eyes radiant.

Grandfather sends a check to Miss Claxton, thanking her for her teaching. With the money, the school purchases a gramophone . . .

. . . and names it Pluto.

Venetia is a hero!

As Venetia grows, Pluto tilts and spins in its long, slow orbit around the sun. It shares the outer reaches of the solar system with other spheres newly discovered by astronomers.

Venetia gets older, and older still. Her hair turns silver.

And one gray July afternoon, the day before her eighty-ninth birthday, she
travels to the Observatory Science Centre, near the southern tip of England.
She has been invited to view Pluto through a telescope—her first time ever.

It's raining, though, and it takes a clear sky to see the dwarf planet.

But as Venetia nears, the rain stops and the clouds begin to part.

A lovely sunset fills the sky.

Later, the darkness twinkling with stars, Venetia and
the scientists climb to the observatory's dome, where
the 111-year-old telescope is waiting. The scientists locate
Pluto, and Venetia puts her eye to the lens.

"By God," she says in an awed voice. There it is, that icy sphere spinning 3.67 billion miles from the sun, many paces past Neptune—and its name is Pluto.

AUTHOR'S NOTE

VENETIA KATHARINE BURNEY was born in Oxford, England, on July 11, 1918. This book closely follows her true life story, including her planet walk at school, her great interest in studying the solar system  and Greek and Roman mythology, and her visit to the Observatory Science Centre when she was older. Venetia did indeed suggest the name Pluto after her grandfather shared the article about the planet's discovery, and the letters from Professor Turner and the astronomers' decision process about the name are historically accurate. When I put these events into the story, I imagined how Venetia waited, and how she reacted when she found out that her name, Pluto, had been chosen.

What happened to Venetia in the years after she named Pluto? She grew up to become an accountant, working with numbers, and later a math and economics teacher, pursuing her love of learning. She married Maxwell Phair, who studied the culture and languages of ancient Greece and Rome. Imagine the conversations they had! Venetia Burney Phair lived until the age of ninety. She died in Surrey, England, on April 30, 2009.

And what about Pluto? As telescopes became stronger, scientists found other icy, rocky objects in the outer reaches of the solar system where Pluto orbits. They named the region the Kuiper Belt. In 2005, an object that appeared to be larger than Pluto was discovered. The discovery of Eris, as it was named, led scientists to rethink the definition of a planet. In 2006, based on that new definition, scientists made the difficult decision to reclassify Pluto as a dwarf planet.

In an interview with NASA, when Venetia was asked whether she was upset by the decision, she responded, "I suppose I would prefer it to remain a planet."

Grandfather Madan understood the importance of Venetia's contribution to science. Along with his check to the school and his letter of thanks to Miss Claxton, he gave Venetia a five-pound note (worth more than three hundred dollars in today's currency) and two scrapbooks of articles about Venetia and Pluto that he'd clipped from newspapers.

Venetia is the only child to have named a planet, and science has honored her for it. In 2006, when NASA launched *New Horizons*—a robotic spacecraft that would fly to Pluto and beyond—on board was an instrument named the Venetia Burney Student Dust Counter. It was the first instrument on a NASA mission designed, built, and operated by students. When *New Horizons* reached Pluto in July 2015, it photographed a large crater-filled area there—which was named Burney Basin.

SELECTED BIBLIOGRAPHY

amblesideonline.org/PR/PR62p030PlanetPluto.shtml (Miss Claxton describing the planet walk; Grandfather's letter to Miss Claxton.)

Jimenez, Ginita, director. *Naming Pluto*. Father Films: 2008. (Documentary film.)

nasa.gov/multimedia/podcasting/transcript_pluto_naming_podcast.html (Interview, Venetia Burney Phair.)

"A New Planet," *The Times* [London, England], March 14, 1930. *The Times* Digital Archive. Accessed March 3, 2016. (Article that Grandfather Madan read in the *London Times*, shortened to fit the text.)

news.bbc.co.uk/2/hi/science/nature/4596246.stm ("The Girl Who Named a Planet," 2006.)

Moore, Patrick. "The Naming of Pluto," *Sky and Telescope*, November, 1984: 400–401. (Excerpts from the text of the telegram sent by Professor Herbert Hall Turner to Grandfather Madan.)

pluto.jhuapl.edu/Multimedia/Science-Photos/image.php?gallery_id=2&image_id=385 (NASA—Burney Basin, photo of Pluto.)

Lacerta

Pegasus

Delphinus

Pisces

Aquila

Aquarius

Piscis
Austrinus

Capricornus